By Sabrina Mesko

HEALING MUDRAS
Yoga for Your Hands
Random House - Original edition

POWER MUDRAS
Yoga Hand Postures for Women
Random House - Original edition

MUDRA - Gestures of POWER
DVD - Sounds True

CHAKRA MUDRAS DVD set
HAND YOGA for Vitality, Creativity and Success
HAND YOGA for Concentration, Love and Longevity

HEALING MUDRAS
Yoga for Your Hands - New Edition

HEALING MUDRAS - New Edition in full color:
Healing Mudras I. ~ For Your Body
Healing Mudras II. ~ For Your Mind
Healing Mudras III. ~ For Your Soul

POWER MUDRAS
Yoga Hand Postures for Women - New Edition

MUDRA THERAPY
Hand Yoga for Pain Management and Conquering Illness

YOGA MIND
45 Meditations for Inner Peace, Prosperity and Protection

MUDRAS for ASTROLOGICAL SIGNS
Volumes I. ~ XII.
MUDRAS for ARIES, TAURUS, GEMINI, CANCER, LEO, VIRGO,
LIBRA, SCORPIO, SAGITTARIUS, CAPRICORN, AQUARIUS, PISCES
12 Book Series

LOVE MUDRAS
Hand Yoga for Two

MUDRAS AND CRYSTALS
The Alchemy of Energy Protection

THE HOLISTIC CAREGIVER
A Guidebook for at-home care in late stage of Alzheimer's and dementia

MUDRAS

for

TAURUS

By Sabrina Mesko Ph.D.H.

The material contained in this book has been written for informational purposes and is not intended as a substitute for medical advice nor is it intended to diagnose, treat, cure, or prevent disease. If you have a medical issue or illness, consult a qualified physician.

A Mudra Hands™ Book
Published by Mudra Hands Publishing

Copyright © 2013 Sabrina Mesko Ph.D.H.

Photography by Mara
Animal photography by Sabrina Mesko
Illustrations by Kiar Mesko
Cover photo by Mara

Printed in the United States of America

ISBN-13:978-0615917610
ISBN-10: 0615917615

For all my Taurus Friends

TABLE OF CONTENTS

THE MUDRA PRACTICE IS A
COMPLIMENTARY HEALING TECHNIQUE,
THAT OFFERS FAST AND EFFECTIVE
POSITIVE RESULTS.

MUDRAS WORK HARMONIOUSLY
WITH OTHER TRADITIONAL,
ALTERNATIVE AND COMPLEMENTARY
HEALING PROTOCOLS.

THEY HELP RESTORE DEPLETED
SUBTLE ENERGY STATES
AND OPTIMIZE THE PRACTITIONER'S
OVERALL STATE OF WELLNESS.

Mudras for TAURUS

APRIL 21 - MAY 21

BODY
Throat, neck, thyroid

PLANET
Venus

COLORS
Pastel Blue, green, pink

ELEMENT
Earth

STONES and GEMS
Emerald

ANIMAL
Cattle

INTRODUCTION

Ever since I can remember, I have been fascinated by the never ending view of the stars in the sky and the presence of other mysterious planets. As a child I wondered for hours about where does the Universe end and when my Father explained the possibility that time and space exist in a very different way than we imagined, my mind went wild with possibilities. I was however quite skeptical about astrology in general until one day in my early youth, a dear friend introduced me to a true Master of Vedic Astrology. He quickly and completely diminished any of my doubts about how precise certain facts can be revealed in one's Celestial map.

It was as if an invisible veil had been removed, and I was granted a peek over to the other side. The astrologer also adamantly pointed out that nothing is written in stone and one's destiny has a lot of space to navigate thru. You can make the best of the situation if you know your given parameters. My fascination and use of astrological science continues to this day and compliments and enriches my work with other observation techniques that I use when consulting.

One is born with character aspects and potential for realization of mapped-out future events, but there is always a possibility that another road may be taken. This has to do with the choices we make. Free will is given to all of us, even though often the choices we have seem to be very limited. But still, the choices are always there, forcing us to consciously participate and eventually take responsibility for our decisions, actions, and consequences.

The science of Astrology has been around for millenniums and even though some people are still doubtful, I always remind them that there is no disputing the fact, that the Moon affects the high and low tide of our Oceans - hence our bodies consisting mostly of water are affected by planetary movements in many fascinating and profound ways. Even the biggest skeptic agrees with that fact.

The Love of the Universal Power for each one of us is unconditional, everlasting and omnipresent. No matter what kind of life-journey you have, it is the very best one designed especially for you, rest assured. And when you are experiencing life's various challenges and wishing for a smooth ride instead, keep in mind that a life filled with lessons is a life fulfilling its purpose. The tests you encounter in your daily life are your opportunities. The wisdom learned is your asset, and the experiences gained are your wealth. Your Spirit's abundance is measured by the battles you fought and how you fought them. Did you help others and leave this world a better place in any way? Your true intention matters more than you know.

Each one of us has a very unique-one of a kind celestial map placed gently, but firmly and irrevocably into effect at the precise time of our birth. There are certain aspects of one's chart that reveal possible character tendencies and predisposed behavior in regards to love, partnerships, maintaining one's health, pursuit of success and a way of communicating. The benefits of knowing and understanding the effects of your chart on various aspects of your life can be profound. It can help you understand and prepare ahead of time for certain circumstances that are coming your way, which increases the possibility of a better quality of life in general.

If you knew that a specific time period could be beneficial for your career wouldn't it be good to know that ahead of your plans? If you are aware that certain aspects of your physical constitution are predisposed to a weakness or sensitivity, wouldn't it be beneficial to pay attention and prevent a possible future health ailment?

If you can foresee that a certain time will be slower for you in achieving positive results, wouldn't it be wise to use that time for preparation for a more fortuitous timing? How many times have you attempted to pursue a dream of yours that just didn't seem to want to happen? And when you were completely exhausted and disillusioned, the fortunate opportunity presented itself, except now you were tired, overwhelmed and had no energy or enthusiasm left. Having such information ahead of time would offer you the chance to save your energy during quiet, less active time, so that when your luck is more likely, you can seize the opportunity and make the most of it. Since writing my first books on Mudras a while ago, my work has expanded into many different areas, however I always included Mudras into my new ventures. When I designed International Wellness and Spa centers, I included Mudra programs to share these beneficial techniques with a wide audience. I included Mudras into my weekly TV show and guided large audiences thru practice on live shows.

Mudras will forever fascinate me and I have been humbled and excited how many practitioners from around the world have written me, grateful to have these techniques and most importantly really experiencing positive effects in time of need. Therefore it has been a natural idea for me to combine these two of my favorite topics and create a series of Mudra sets for all twelve Astrological signs.

The Mudras depicted in this book are specifically selected for the astrological sign of ~~Aries~~ with intention to help you maximize your gifts and soften the challenges that your celestial map contains.

It is important to know that each astrological chart - celestial map-contains information that can be used beneficially and there are no "bad signs" or "better sings". Your chart is unique as are you. By gaining information, knowledge and understanding what the placements of the planets offer you, your path to self knowledge is strengthened.

I hope this book will attract astrology readers as well as meditation and yoga practitioners and help you utilize the beneficial combination of both these fascinating techniques. Knowledge will help you experience the very best possible version of your life. The biggest mystery in your life is You. Discover who you are and enjoy the journey.

And remember, no matter what life presents you with, don't forget to smile and keep a happy heart. With each experience gained you are spiritually wealthier for it. And that my friend, stays with you forever.

The wisdom gained is eternally imprinted in your soul.

Blessings,

Sabrina

MUDRAS

Mudras are movements involving only fingers, hands and arms. Mudras originated in ancient Egypt where they were practiced by high priests and priestesses in sacred rituals. Mudras can be found in every culture of the world. We all use Mudras in our everyday life when gesturing while communicating and when holding our hands in various intuitive positions. Mudras used in yoga practice offer great benefits and have a tremendously positive overall effect on our overall state of well-being. By connecting specific fingertips and your palms in various Mudra positions, you are directly affecting complex energy currents of your subtle energy body. As numerous energy currents run thru your brain centers, Mudras help stimulate specific areas for an overall state of emotional, physical and mental well being.

INSTRUCTIONS FOR MUDRA PRACTICE

YOUR BODY POSTURE
During the Mudra practice sit in an upright position with a straight spine, with both your feet on the ground or in a cross legged position. Comfort is essential so that you may practice undisturbed and focus on proper practice positions.

YOUR EYES
Keep your eyes closed and gently lightly lift the gaze above the horizon.

WHERE
For achieving best results of ideal Mudra practice it is essential that you find a peaceful place, without distractions. Once your Mudra practice is established, you can practice Mudras anywhere.

WHEN
You may practice Mudras at any time. Best times for practice are first thing in the morning and at bedtime. Avoid practicing Mudras on a full stomach, and after a big meal wait for an hour before practice.

HOW LONG
Each Mudra should be practiced for at least 3 minutes at a time. Ideal practice is 3 Mudras for 3 minutes each with a follow up short 3 minutes of complete stillness, peace and meditation or reflection.

HOW OFTEN
You may practice Mudras every day. Explore various Mudras by selecting a Mudra that fits your specific needs for any given day.

BREATH CONTROL
Proper breathing is essential for optimal Mudra practice. There are two main breathing techniques that can be used with your practice.

LONG DEEP SLOW BREATH
Slowly and deeply inhale thru your nose while relaxing and expanding the area or your solar plexus and lower stomach. Exhale thru the nose slowly while gently contracting the stomach area and pulling your stomach in. Pace your breathing slowly and notice the immediate calming effects. This breathing technique is appropriate for relaxation, inducing calmness and peace.

BREATH OF FIRE
Inhale and exhale thru the nose at a much faster pace while practicing the same concept of expanding navel area and contracting with each exhalation. Unless otherwise noted Mudras are generally practiced with the long slow breath.The breath of fire has an energizing, recharging effect on body and is to be used only when so noted.

CHAKRAS

Along our spine, starting at the base and continuing up towards the top of your head, lie subtle energy centers-vortexes-called charkas, that have a powerful effect on the overall state of your health and well being.
The practice of Mudras profoundly affects the proper function of these energy centers and magnifies their power.

Our subtle energy body is highly sensitive to outside sensory stimuli of sound, aromas, visuals and outside electric currents that constantly surround us. Frequencies that permeate specific locations may attract or bother you. Perhaps you may feel eager to stay somewhere where the energy suits you and yet feel suffocated when the environment does not agree with you. We are all sensitive to energies, but some of us feel them more than others.

A positive blend of energies with another person can create a magnet-like effect, whereas another person's negative unharmonious subtle energy field subconsciously pushes you away.

By leading healthy lives and optimizing the proper function of charkas, you empower your subtle energy bodies adding strength to your physical body, mind and spirit. Destructive behavior like addictions and abuse weakens your Auric field and "leaks" your vital energy. By maintaining a healthy Aura-energy field, you can fine-tune your natural capacity for "sensing" places, situations and people that compliment your energy frequency.
In a state of "clean energy" you achieve capacity for high awareness and become your own best guide.

CHAKRAS IN THE BODY

Base Chakra: Foundation
Second Chakra: Sexuality
Third Chakra: Ego
Fourth Chakra: Love
Fifth Chakra: Truth
Sixth Chakra: Intuition
Seventh Chakra: Divine Wisdom

FIRST CHAKRA
LOCATION: Base of the spine
GLAND: Gonad
COLOR: Red
REPRESENTS:
Foundation, shelter, survival,
courage, inner security, vitality

SECOND CHAKRA
LOCATION: Sex organs
GLAND: Adrenal
COLOR: Orange
REPRESENTS:
Creative expression, sexuality,
procreation, family

THIRD CHAKRA
LOCATION: Solar plexus
GLAND: Pancreas
COLOR: Yellow
REPRESENTS:
Ego, intellect, emotions of fear and anger

FOURTH CHAKRA
LOCATION: Heart
GLAND: Thymus
COLOR: Green
REPRESENTS:
All matters of the heart, love,
self–love, compassion and faith

FIFTH CHAKRA

LOCATION: Throat
GLAND: Thyroid
COLOR: Blue
REPRESENTS:
Communication, truth,
higher knowledge, your voice

SIXTH CHAKRA

LOCATION: Third Eye
GLAND: Pineal
COLOR: Indigo
REPRESENTS:
Intuition, inner vision, the Third eye

SEVENTH CHAKRA

LOCATION: Top of the head - Crown
GLAND: Pituitary
COLOR: White and Violet
REPRESENTS:
The universal God consciousness,
the heavens, unity

NADIS

Your subtle energy body contains an amazing network of electric currents called Nadis. There are 72.000 energy currents that run throughout your body from toes to the top of your head as well as your fingertips. These channels of light must be clear and vibrant with life force for your optimal health and empowerment. With regular Mudra practice you can open, clear, reactivate and re-energize your energy currents.

Your Hands and Fingers

While practicing Mudras you are magnifying the effects of the Solar system on your physical, mental and spiritual body. Each finger is influenced by the following planets:

THE THUMB - MARS

THE INDEX FINGER - JUPITER

THE MIDDLE FINGER - SATURN

THE RING FINGER – THE SUN

THE LITTLE FINGER - MERCURY

MANTRA

Combining the Mudra practice with appropriate Mantras magnifies the beneficial effects of these ancient self-healing techniques.

The hard palate in your mouth has 58 energy meridian points that connect to and affect your entire body.

By singing, speaking or whispering Mantras, you touch these energy points in a specific order that is beneficial and has a harmonious and healing effect on your physical, mental and spiritual state.

The ancient science of Mantras helps you reactivate nadis, magnifies and empowers your energy field, improves your concentration and stills your mind.

About Astrology

The word Horoscope originates from a Latin word ORA–hour and SCOPOS–view. One could presume that Horoscope means "a look into your hour of birth". The precise moment of your birth determines your celestial set-up.

An accurate astrological chart can reveal most detailed aspects of your life, your character, your gifts, your future possible events, challenges that await you, lucky events that are bestowed upon you, and your outlook for happy relationships, successful careers, accomplishments, health and many possible variations of life events. I say possible, because your decisions will determine the outcome.

There are 12 signs in the Zodiac and your birth-day reflects the position of your Sun sign. The specific positions of other planets in your chart are calculated considering the precise moment-hour and minute and of course location of your birth. The birth time will reveal your Rising or Ascending sign, which will further determine other essential facts of your chart.

The constant transitional movements of the Planets affect each one of us differently, a time that may be difficult for some may prove supremely lucky for another and yet we are interconnected by mutual effects of continuous planetary movements. Nothing is standing still, the changes are ongoing. On a different note, a few slow moving planets connect us in other ways, as they keep certain generations under specific aspects and influences. We are all inseparable and in continuous motion.

There are numerous fascinating ways to use astrology and there is no doubt that the constant motion of all these powerful and majestic Planets in our Solar system affect each and every one of us differently. Astrology can be used as an additional tool to help you continue progressing on the mysterious life journey of self discovery and self-realization.

Remember, the power of decision is yours as is the responsibility for consequences. Make peace with your doubts, pursue your dreams and relish in results.

When the outcome is less than what you expected, learn to pick yourself up and continue on, wiser with knowledge you gained, that alone being a good reason for remaining optimistic. When the outcome surpasses your expectations, well, then you will know what to do… mostly take a breath, smile, and enjoy the moment.

YOUR SUN SIGN

There are 12 signs in the Zodiac. The day of your birth determines your Sun-sign. Most often this is the extent of average person's knowledge and interest in astrology. However, the other aspects in the astrological chart are equally as important and need to be taken into consideration. In this book your main guide is your Sun sign's dispositions, tendencies, weaknesses and gifts. Certainly there are endless combinations of charts and your Sun sign alone will not reveal the complete picture of your celestial map.

For more detailed information and reflection about your chart, you need to know your ascending-rising sign.

Your Ascending-Rising Sign

Your rising sign, also known as the ascendant, reflects the degree of ecliptic rising over the eastern horizon at the precise moment of your birth. It reveals the foundation of your personality. That means that even if you have the same birthday with someone else, your time of birth would create completely different aspects and influences in your chart. No two people are alike. You are one of a kind and so is everyone else. However, you may have some strong similarities and timing aspects that will be often alike. Your rising sign also reveals the basis of your chart and House placements. Your rising sign determines and is in your first house. There are 12 Houses and each depicts precise in-depth information about all aspects of your physical life, emotional make and character tendencies. It is incredibly complex and fascinating. Regarding your Mudra practice in combination with your Astrological Sign, it would be beneficial to know also your Rising sign and apply Mudras that empower your Rising sign as well. For example; if your Sun sign is Aries, but your rising sign is Libra-it would be most beneficial to practice Mudra sets for both signs.

How to use this book

In each book of the *Mudras for the Astrological Signs* series, you will find Mudras for different astrological signs that will help you in most important areas of your life: Health, Love, Success, and Overcoming your challenging qualities. We all have them, as we also all have gifts. This book is specific for the sign of Taurus. You may change your Mudra practice daily as needed, and keep in mind, that certain habits or tendencies need a longer time to adjust, change, and improve. Be patient, kind, and loving towards yourself.

Mudras for Transcending Challenges

Each one of us has a few character tendencies or weaknesses that are connected to our astrological chart. To help you transcend, overcome and redirect these challenges into your beneficial assets, you can use the Mudras in this chapter.

Mudras for Health and Beauty

Each astrological sign rules certain areas of your body. The Mudras in this chapter will help you strengthen your physical weaknesses while maintaining a healthy body, and a beautiful, vibrant appearance.

Mudras for Love

The Mudras in this chapter will help you understand your love temperament, your expectations, your longings and how to attract the optimal love partner into your life. It is most beneficial to know how others perceive you in the matters of the heart. It will also help you understand your partner and their astrologically influenced love map.

Mudras for Success

The Mudras in this chapter will offer you tools to present yourself to the world in your optimal light. Often one is confused in which direction to turn or where their strength lies. Mudras will help you focus and remember your essential creative desires, help you gain self-confidence and inner security to recognize your desired and destined path. If you know what you want, and your purpose is harmonious for the better good of all, your success is within reach.

MUDRAS
for TRANSCENDING CHALLENGES

MUDRA FOR
POWERFUL INSIGHT

Your determined nature is often the driving force and the reason behind your much desired success. But on every road there are circumstances that slow us down. Sometimes these unplanned stops are very necessary learning experiences. No matter how brilliant you are, there will come a time sooner or latter that you will be mistaken about something. Yet, admitting to being wrong is one of those impossible things for you that you very much dislike. It is extremely difficult for you not to claim victory. But remember, you will loose much less energy, if you wisely admit to your error and quickly move on. Yes, it is a humbling experience and no one likes it, but you can avoid this uncomfortable scenario, by carefully assessing a situation ahead of time. Practice this Mudra and it will help you recognize a possible mistake. Then, you can cleverly adjust your approach and emerge wise and victorious - your favorite outcome.

CHAKRA: 6

COLOR: Indigo

Sit with a straight back, elbows out to either side. Raise your hands until they meet above the navel point. The back of the left hand rests in the right palm and the thumbs are crossed, left over right.

BREATH: Long, deep and slow.

MUDRA FOR
MEDITATION OF CHANGE

You love your home and there is nothing more appealing to you than a cozy snugly evening in your plush environment. You dislike being taken away from your precious and special home. You also are not very fond of change in general, especially under rushed circumstances. But life is full of surprises and your home-bound attitude could be holding you back.

It is also important to realize and accept that every good thing in life came with a change as well. Therefore it is very beneficial for you to accept, welcome, and not delay necessary change. This Mudra will help you relax, accept and sail smoothly through life's changes. Dare to be adventurous!

CHAKRA: 6, 7

COLOR: Indigo, violet

MANTRA:
ONG NAMO GURUDEV NAMO
(I bow to the Infinite Creative Consciousness
and Divine Wisdom)

Sit with a straight back. Curl the fingers into fists, the fingertips pressing in the upper pads of the hands. Connect the hands of all knuckles and the pads of the thumbs. The thumbs are extended and the fingertips touching. The connected hands are held in front of the navel with thumbs directed slightly upwards towards your heart. Hold and concentrate on the energy in your hands.

BREATH: Long, deep and slow.

MUDRA for
Evoking Inner STRENGTH

Oh yes, those comfortable and luxurious days that you so adore. There is no secret about the lifestyle you seek and enjoy. But there is also a slight tendency to get too comfortable and laid back and dare we say, maybe a tiny bit lazy. Well, it happens to the best of us, but for those days when you know you just must get yourself together and snap out of that comfy zone, this Mudra will help you gather the inner power and engage in some productive activity.

After all, you are in this world to accomplish something as well, and if you want to continue to enjoy that luxurious home environment, you need to get busy.

CHAKRA: 3, 4

COLOR: Yellow, Green

Sit with a straight back. Curl your index fingers and curl your thumbs over them. Straighten the other three fingers. Your right hand is slightly under the left hand, your middle two finger pads touching the joints of the left hand. Place your hands in front of your chest, keeping the elbows up out out the sides so that your forearms and hands make lines parallel to the ground.

BREATH: Inhale thru the nose and shape your lips into an O, and exhale with a whistle.

MUDRAS for HEALTH and BEAUTY

MUDRA FOR A POWERFUL VOICE

Your sign rules the voice and neck area. Thyroid is also under Taurus influence therefore it is most important to keep yourself strong and healthy in that aspect. Proper diet, exercise, and healthy lifestyle are a must. This Mudra will help you activate, recharge and enhance your communication skills, and who knows-you may even start singing beautiful arias in the shower. On a more serious note, it is most important to know how to communicate your power to the rest of the world, be it personal or professional in nature.

CHAKRA: 5

COLOR: Blue

Sit with a straight back. Place your hands in front of your chest, palms apart and all fingertips touching. All fingers are spread apart. Inhale and press together the thumbs and the index fingers. Exhale and relax. Now inhale and press together the thumbs and the middle fingers. Exhale and relax. Continue the same way with the ring and little fingers. Practice for three minutes and finish up the cycle.

BREATH: Long, deep and slow.

MUDRA
FOR RECHARGING

You are very fond of creature comforts and love luxury. One of your favorite things is to get pampered and have plenty of time for rest and relaxation. It is therefore every important for your entire being that you take full advantage of any free time you have. Maybe you just have few minutes a day when you can steal away and enjoy some peace. You need a quick pick me up. This Mudra is excellent for that occasion and will help you recharge within minutes. You will feel as if you've been resting an entire afternoon. Visualize a beautiful place in nature while practicing this Mudra and replenish your body, mind and spirit.

CHAKRA: 1, 2, 7

COLOR: Red, orange, violet

Sit with a straight back. Extend your arms straight out in front of you, parallel to the ground. Make a fist with your right hand. Wrap your left fingers around the fist, with the bases of the palms touching, thumbs close together and extended straight up.

BREATH: Long, deep and slow.

MUDRA FOR REJUVENATION

You love all things of beauty and have exquisite taste. That is one of the reasons that you love to surround yourself with beautiful people, things, art or other material belongings. Preservation of your stunning appearance is quite important to you and you are master of all things that make one beautiful. If a new product that guarantees to preserve your youthful appearance just arrived on the market, you will be the one to know about it first. You also hate being rushed and could be very comfortable lounging timelessly in a spa. This Mudra will offer you just what you need. It will instantly rejuvenate you and soothe your senses with the ocean-like hush that you create while massaging your ears. Close your eyes and imagine you are sitting at the edge of an ocean. Time and pressure don't exist. Breathe and enjoy.

CHAKRA: 5, 6, 7

COLOR: Blue, indigo, violet

MANTRA:
OM
(God in His Absolute State)

Sit with a straight back. Place both palms of your hands directly on your ears. Circle your hands and massage your ears in a circular motion in the direction away from your face-counter clockwise. Listen to the sound of "*the ocean*" that you are creating with your hands.

BREATH: Long, deep and slow.

MUDRAS
for LOVE

MUDRA for Higher CONSCIOUSNESS

While you are a lover that knows how to experience romance in true sense of the word, create a dream romantic fantasy environment, and mesmerize your partner, you also posses the capacity to quickly loose your temper. All the romance flies out the window instantly. It is therefore very important, to be able to elevate and extract yourself from the situation that is upsetting you, and employ your higher awareness to help you see what is the real reason for disharmony. It may be your overprotective character that is limiting the freedom your loved one needs to feel. Before you let your temper get the best of you, distance yourself from the situation for a few minutes and practice this Mudra. Within moments you will see a possible other aspect to the situation and find a harmonious solution.

CHAKRA: 3, 7

COLOR: Blue, violet

MANTRA:
OM
(God in His Absolute State)

Sit with a straight back. Put your palms together and extend your elbows to either side. Lift your hands in front of your heart, fingers pointed away from you. Each thumb is on the fleshy mound below the little finger of the same hand. Put the palms together with the right thumb snugly above the left thumb. The bottoms of the hands touch firmly. Hold the hands a few inches away from the body.

BREATH: Long, deep and slow.

MUDRA of TRUTH

Your tendency to be secretive can work both ways. You may be able to create an amazing surprise, keep the deep secrets of your best friend, and never let anyone know about it. Or you may keep some secrets from your loved one. Sometimes is a real relief to finally let the truth be revealed and just be yourself. Being able to confide in your lover will bring you closer and tighter. Leaving them out may create an unwanted distance. You need to be courageous to tell the truth and that is not always the easiest thing in the world. This Mudra will help you feel confident and find the best approach to speak out, be honest and truthful, and release a deep secret. Chances are it will help your lover do the same which will deepen your bond. Give it a try.

CHAKRA: 6

COLOR: Violet

MANTRA:
EK ONG KAR
(One Creator, God is One)

Sit with a straight back. Bend your elbows and lift your arms up so that the elbows are parallel to the ground. Palms are facing out and all fingers are together. Hold for three minutes.

BREATH: Long, deep and slow.

MUDRA FOR TRUST

Trust is the fundamental strength in every relationship. But first you must trust yourself. The ultimate trust is the trust in the creative Universal energy that is a part of every and each one of us. Trust that everything happens at the right time, that there is an amazing individual plan for every one of us, and trust that you will meet the love of your life when you least expect it. Your stubborn nature sometimes argues with this trust and wants things it's way. Release this tendency or at least soften it up a bit, so that you may be able to enjoy life's surprises including the most delicious one of falling in love and meeting your match. If the person does not fit your fixed idea of the "perfect one", take a deep breath, relax and trust. You will be surprised. It turns out, someone knows you better than you know yourself.

CHAKRA: 7

COLOR: Violet

MANTRA:
HAR HAR HAR WAHE GURU
(God's Creation, His Supreme power and Wisdom)

Sit with a straight back. Make a circle with your arms arched up over your head, palms down. Put the right palm on top of the left. Lightly press the thumb tips together, keep your back straight and visualize a circle of white   protective light around you.

BREATH: Short, fast, breath of fire focusing on the navel. Practice for a minute and relax with deep slow breath for another two minutes.

MUDRAS
for SUCCESS

MUDRA FOR A SHARP MIND

In order to pursue a successful life, you need to develop a very necessary quality of a sharp and quick mind. Knowing what you want and how to make your way towards your goal is essential. When you forget about exercising the mind like a fine musical instrument, you forget how powerful you really are. It is all in the mind. You tend to lead others with your business expertise. Take your natural tendency to a higher level and guide your determined nature so that you won't waste precious energy. While you are very ambitious, it is wise to reflect on all your options before going forward full force. Take a moment for yourself, breathe, relax and focus your mind with this Mudra.

CHAKRA: 5, 6

COLOR: Blue, indigo

MANTRA:
HARA HARE HARI
(The Creator in Action)

Sit with a straight back. Hold the left hand up as though to clap, then with the index and middle fingers of the right hand slowly and with strong pressure walk up the center of the left palm to the very tips of the middle and ring fingers. Walk up as you inhale and down as you exhale.

BREATH: Long, deep and slow.

MUDRA FOR
RELEASING NEGATIVE EMOTIONS

No matter what the circumstances are and how right you may be, it is never wise to loose temper in a business environment. Your stubborn nature may push you into a corner that may prove challenging to get out of. Don't ignore the danger of drowning just because you won't admit the water is too deep. When you are bursting with negative emotions, find a quite place where you can have a few moments alone and release the negativity. You will emerge more powerful and focused. To loose temper means to lose control over yourself. That is something that will never reflect strength in any way. Center yourself and collect the inner power that will allow you to become the powerhouse you were born to become. This Mudra will help you along.

CHAKRA: 4

COLOR: Green

Sit with a straight back. Bend your arms and make fists with both hands. Bring them up in front of your heart. Cross the hands over each other, palms turned outwards. Hold the Mudra across the chest with the left arm on the outer side.

BREATH: Long, deep and slow.

MUDRA FOR
INNER INTEGRITY

Knowing yourself and your good as well as weaker habits is empowering. Being able to admit that you are wrong may be difficult, but the longer you delay that realization, the more painful the ending. It shows great strength of character and self esteem when you recognize and admit your error. Every successful person failed many times before succeeding and certainly we've all been wrong at times. We improve and learn from past mistakes. So take a deep breath and empower yourself with the truth. By admitting your weaknesses like the love of extreme comfort and maybe a trace of laziness, you are making a great first step towards change, but only if you make that choice. Stay true to your heart and pure ideas, and your success will manifest, rest assured.

CHAKRA: 4

COLOR: Green

Sit with a straight back. Bend your elbows and lift your upper arms parallel to the ground. Bring your hands to ear level, palms facing out. Curl the fingers inward and point the thumbs out toward your ears. Hold for three minutes and relax.

BREATH: Short, fast, breath of fire from the navel.

ABOUT THE AUTHOR

SABRINA MESKO   PH.D.H. is an International and Los Angeles Times bestselling author of the timeless classic *Healing Mudras - Yoga for your Hands* translated into fourteen languages. She authored over twenty books on Mudras, Mudra Therapy, Mudras and Astrology, Holistic Caregiving, Spirituality and Meditation techniques.

Sabrina holds a Bachelors Degree in Sensory Approaches to Healing, a Masters in Holistic Science, a Doctorate in Ancient and Modern Approaches to Healing, and a Ph.D.H in Healtheoloyy from the American Institute of Holistic Theology. She is board certified from the American Alternative medical Association and American Holistic Health Association. She has been featured in media outlets such as The Los Angeles Times, CNBC News, Cosmopolitan, the cover of London Times Lifestyle, The Discovery Channel documentary on Hands, W magazine, First for Women, Health, Web-MD, Daily News, Focus, Yoga Journal, Australian Women's weekly, Blend, Daily Breeze, New Age, the Roseanne Show and various international live television programs. Her articles have been published in world-wide publications. She hosted her own weekly TV show educating about health, well-being and complementary medicine. She is an executive member of the World Yoga Council and has led numerous international Yoga Therapy educational programs. She directed and produced her interactive double DVD titled   *Chakra Mudras* - a Visionary awards finalist.

Sabrina also created award winning international Spa and Wellness Centers and is a motivational keynote conference speaker addressing large audiences all over the world. She is the founder of Arnica Press, a boutique Book Publishing House. Her mission is to discover, mentor, nurture and publish unique authors with a meaningful message, that may otherwise not have an opportunity to be heard. She is the founder of world's only online Mudra Teacher and Mudra Therapy Education, Certification and Mentorship program, with her certified therapists spreading these ancient teachings in over 27 countries around the world.

www.SabrinaMesko.com